JULIA
MARGARET
CAMERON

JULIA MARGARET CAMERON

Margaret Harker

COLLINS

JULIA MARGARET CAMERON

by Margaret Harker

Julia Margaret Cameron is photography's great eccentric. She flouted the conventions of her day, not deliberately but quite unselfconsciously when she found them restrictive or merely irksome. She was completely undaunted by the dictates of the polite society of the period in which she lived. She was an individual spirit in an era which promoted individualism and yet she still found inspiration in the works of artists and literary men whom she highly respected. In this sense she was a product of the Victorian age in which she lived.

Born on 11 June 1815, at Garden Reach, Calcutta, India and christened Julia Margaret, she was the third daughter of James Pattle, a Scotsman who was a highly placed official in the Bengal Civil Service, and his French wife, Adeline de l'Etang, whose parents were French aristocrats. Julia, with six of her eight sisters (there was only one brother), was brought up by their French maternal grandmother, Madame de Grincourt, but they received the final part of their education in England. Their home was in India. All the sisters inherited a well developed aesthetic sense and good taste from their mother's side of the family. They all made socially 'good' marriages, in most instances to men in high positions in the British Army or Civil Service in India.

At the age of twenty-one Julia Pattle met her future husband, Charles Hay Cameron, at the Cape of Good Hope where each had been sent to recover from ill-health. During this recuperation she also met Sir John Herschel, the celebrated astronomer who was involved in the invention of photography. He coined the terms 'negative' and 'positive' and was responsible for discovering the properties of sodium thiosulphate (hypo) as a most efficient fixing agent for the final stage of processing photographs. They became firm friends and years later when Mrs Cameron took up photography as a serious pursuit she turned to Sir John Herschel for advice on technical matters.

In 1838 Julia Pattle married Charles Hay Cameron, who was 20 years older than her, his second wife. He was a jurist and a fine classical scholar and from 1843 to 1848 he served as the legal member of the Council of India. The Camerons resided in Calcutta. He invested in coffee plantations in Ceylon.

Julia Margaret Cameron became distinguished in Anglo-Indian society for her brilliant conversation and ready wit. In the absence of the wife of the Governor General of India, Lord Hardinge, Mrs Cameron became leader of the European social set when she was barely 30. She shared her husband's humanitarian principles and aims and had a distaste for the excessively formal conventions in Anglo-Indian society. Her personality and individuality of outlook led to the relaxation of rigid patterns of behaviour, at least in her presence, but in order to combat the over-zealous conventionalists she developed an imperious manner on which friends and acquaintances passed comment in the more relaxed social atmosphere of English homes. In the 1840s her talents, in addition to being a brilliant hostess, found outlets in translating Bürger's ballad *Lenore* from German into English and in writing poetry, one or two of which were published at a later date in *Macmillan's Magazine*.

In 1848, when Charles Cameron retired from fulltime service in India, the family took up residence in England at Ephraim Court, Tunbridge Wells, Kent. After two years the Camerons moved house to East Sheen in Surrey and from there to Putney Heath, London.

During the years in London Julia Cameron frequently visited her sister, Sarah

Prinsep, and her husband who resided at Little Holland House in Kensington, London. The Prinseps kept brilliant company, entertaining famous literary people and artists such as Alfred, Lord Tennyson, the Poet Laureate; Robert Browning, an equally distinguished poet; George Frederick Watts, the painter, who visited in 1851 for three days and was persuaded to stay for twenty three years; as well as statesmen and scholars. At the dinner table one could be seated next to Thackeray, Rossetti, Burne-Jones, Whistler, Millais, Lord Leighton, Holman Hunt, Ruskin or Sir John Herschel.

In 1860 the Camerons again moved house, this time to Dimbola—a 'cottage style' residence named after Charles' coffee plantations in the Dimbula valley, Ceylon—in the locality of Freshwater Bay, Isle of Wight, a short journey by boat from Southampton. In 1863 when Charles Cameron was on one of his periodic visits to his estates in Ceylon and the children were grown up (her sons in India and her daughter married), Julia became very depressed through inactivity and a loss of direction in her life. To cheer her up her daughter, also named Julia, and son-in-law, Charles Norman, presented her with a large wooden camera, a Jamin lens and a darkroom outfit with the words: 'It may amuse you, Mother, to try to photograph during your solitude at Freshwater.'

Julia Margaret Cameron was then 48, so that her daughter and son-in-law could not possibly have foreseen the remarkable career which followed in the wake of their gifts. The moment was opportune as her time was no longer occupied with family concerns. She had a good aesthetic sense, a lively interest in the arts, especially painting, poetry and drama; extraordinary energy and enthusiasm which she devoted to activities which really interested her; and an inexhaustible supply of 'great men' and 'fair women' within her large circle of relatives, friends and acquaintances on which to draw for sitters. With Sir John Herschel to advise her she mastered the difficult collodion process sufficiently well in a matter of months to produce her first successful portrait, in January 1864. (This process required skill and patience and involved coating a glass plate with collodion—gun-cotton dissolved in ether to which alcohol was added—containing potassium iodide, which was then sensitized in a silver nitrate solution. The plate had to be exposed in the camera while still moist and developed immediately afterwards.)

Mrs Cameron recounted her adventures in photography in *Annals of My Glass House* which she commenced writing in 1874 but unfortunately failed to finish. A friend of the family recalled that, 'The smell of collodion mingled with the scent of sweet briar, copying [printing] frames were spread on the lawn and Mrs Cameron's penetrating voice could be heard giving orders to her maid in the "glass house".' She lacked the patience to become a skilled photographic technician, nor was she interested in the craft of photography but was immensely fascinated by the imagery. She was severely criticised by contemporary photographic practitioners for her careless technique, but lavishly praised by artists and art critics for the pictures she produced.

Criticised by contemporary photographic practitioners . . . but lavishly praised by artists . . .

In spite of her unorthodox behaviour, imperious manner and strange appearance she commanded admiration and affection from friends and was popular with relatives, especially the younger folk. The local children, however, were terrified of being trapped in her studio for hours on end. Edith Nicholl Ellison recalls her childhood impressions in *A Child's Recollections of Tennyson* (published by J.M. Dent in 1907), 'Mrs Cameron was neither mysterious nor awe-inspiring, but just a

5

'Garibaldi thought she was a beggar when she kneeled before him, begging to be allowed to take his picture,' said Mrs Tennyson.

kind, exacting though benevolent, tyrant. Children loved but fled from her. I can see her now, clad in the never-failing wrapper, stained—as were her hands and eager face—with the chemicals she used in her work, her hair falling any way but the right way, lying in wait some fine morning at her garden gate for the young ones passing down the road on their way to Farringford or to the sands of Freshwater Bay. "She's coming! She'll catch one of us!" And sure enough an arm would intercept the passage of some luckless wight, and, bribed by jars of preserve or other toothsome dainty, the victim was led away to spend the sunny hours posing in the studio . . . Undoubtedly Mrs Cameron was a genius in her own way. But she certainly was a strange looking figure, and it was no wonder that, as Mrs Tennyson tells in her diary, Garibaldi thought she was a beggar when she kneeled before him, her stained hands upraised, begging to be allowed to take his picture.'

Rachel and Laura Gurney were great nieces of Julia Cameron (the grandchildren of her sister Sarah Prinsep) and were models for several of her 'angel' and 'cherub' pictures. Her photograph of them as *Rachel and Laura* is a most delightful study of two young children (page 47). It was taken in 1872, but a similar photograph of two other little girls—Kate and Elizabeth 'Topsy' Keown, daughters of a Master Gunner in the Royal Artillary who served at the Freshwater Redoubt not far from Dimbola—was taken as early in Mrs Cameron's career as 1865. This earlier photograph was called *Red and White Roses* (page 12) and may have been a first attempt at illustrating Tennyson's poem *Maud*—the reference being to the White Rose and the Red Rose in 'The Rosebud Garden of Girls'. In 1868 Mrs Cameron took a number of photographs of young women in groups to illustrate this poem (pages 36 and 37). Laura Troubridge (neé Gurney) recollected experiences of posing for Mrs Cameron in *Memories and Reflections* (published by Heinemann, London, in 1925), 'Rachel and I were pressed into the service of the camera. Our roles were no less than those of two angels of the Nativity, and to sustain them we were scantily clad, and each had a pair of heavy swan's wings fastened to her narrow shoulders, while Aunt Julia, with ungentle touch, touzled our hair to get rid of its prim nursery look. No wonder those old photographs of us, leaning over imaginary ramparts of heaven, look anxious and wistful. This is how we felt, for we never knew what Aunt Julia was going to do next, nor did anyone else for the matter of that.'

Mrs Cameron was not alone in her use of swan and duck wings, as an enterprising author of a handbook of photography of the period revealed in an article entitled *Angel Pictures*. This provided a recipe for the procurement, drying and preparation of ducks' wings for photographers (Paul Hasluck: *Book of Photography,* published by Cassell and Company in 1895). *Venus Chiding Cupid and Removing His Wings* (page 48) and *The Nestling Angel* (page 49) are two of Mrs Cameron's best illustrations of this kind. The latter can be compared with the painting by G.F. Watts, *Death Crowning Innocence* (page 48), which is an instance where the picture construction chosen by Watts may have been based on one of Mrs Cameron's ideas. In both photograph and painting 'wings' have been used to encompass the subject; in the former the protective white wings act as shield for the emerging 'nestling angel', whereas in the latter the black wings of death enshroud the group.

During her first two years as a photographer, her imagery was limited by a 'trial and error' approach and by the use of a lens of too short a focal length for portraiture—the images lack the rounded view of the head obtained with a longer focal length lens. The chromatic aberration of her lens—its inability to bring all wavelengths of light to the same point of focus—made definition unpredictable and movement during long exposure times accounted for many failed plates. She was uncertain of how to use lighting to advantage and several of the portraits she took in 1864–66 lack the plasticity of her later work.

The Dirty Monk (page 11), a portrait of Alfred, Lord Tennyson, taken in 1865, is an example of some of these deficiencies. By all accounts the Poet Laureate was a very handsome man and one of Julia Cameron's idols. He was a favourite sitter although he endured the sittings rather than enthused about them. He himself named this early portrait 'The Dirty Monk' which he said was his favourite other than a photograph taken of him by J.E. Mayall, one of the most distinguished professional photographers of the time. The distortion caused by the use of the short focal length lens can be seen in the over-large rendition of the hand. The flat lighting and consequent lack of modelling on the face is uncharacteristic of Mrs Cameron's style as she progressed in her photographic career. However, in spite of these defects it was used by her as the frontispiece in her illustrated version of Tennyson's *Idylls of the King* in 1874.

She made no secret of her intense admiration for Alfred, Lord Tennyson.

Of all the photographs she took of Alfred Tennyson the most successful is that on page 28. Carlyle described him as 'one of the finest looking men in the world. A great shock of rough, dusky, dark hair; bright laughing hazel eyes; massive aquiline face, most massive yet most delicate.' Although Julia Cameron undoubtedly strove hard to do justice to the inner man as well as to the physical description quoted here, the portrait is not in the same category as the two Herschel studies (pages 23 and 25), the two portraits of Carlyle (pages 20 and 21) and the magnificent photograph of Sir Henry Taylor (page 27) which represent the summit of her achievement. Nevertheless she succeeded in capturing a glimpse of his shrewdness and gives an impression of his intelligent strength. She made no attempt to disguise the suit he was wearing. That factor, together with the fulsome lighting and half-length study (as opposed to a 'close-up'), aligns this portrait with the best professional work of the period.

Although Mrs Cameron held an exhibition of her photographs at Colnaghi's, the London print sellers, in 1865 (one year after her 'first success), her remarkable talent was not fully in evidence until late in 1866. By then she was using a camera and lens much better suited to her purpose, she had developed a fine judgement in lighting, and was the better able to command her sitters to pose and retain the expression she required.

It is not without significance that her friends amongst artists and authors were men rather than women. She had several traits of character traditionally associated with men such as her aggressive tendencies and outspokeness. Her work has a virile quality rather than the delicacy and discretion to be expected of a Victorian middle-aged matron. In relationships, however innocent, she invariably made the first move. She made no secret of her intense admiration for Alfred, Lord Tennyson, her adoration of her 'guru', G.F. Watts, and she idolized Sir Henry Taylor, which amused him but embarrassed his wife. For her mentor, Sir John Herschel, she felt deep and lasting affection and she wrote to him frequently and at great length on the subject of her photography.

Other of her characteristics found expression in her photographs. She exaggerated descriptions of events and everyday facts, and tended to over-react to

The full face study of Sir John Herschel . . . arguably her greatest masterpiece.

situations. Life seems to have been one dramatic event after another. A quiet spell left her bored and frustrated. These tendencies are reflected in her dramatic portrayals of many of the great men who were in her sister's circle of friends. She penetrated the veil of reserve, characteristic of most nineteenth century English gentlemen, and exposed the restless genius of Sir John Herschel (pages 23, 24 and 25) whom she photographed at his Collingwood residence on 7 April 1867. She demanded that his hair be washed before taking his photograph to reveal the fluffy whiteness of his tousled locks. The results of this sitting were three superb photographs, each an interpretation of different facets of his character.

The full face study (page 25) is arguably her greatest masterpiece, providing insights to Herschel's intellectual stature and spiritual strength as well as revealing his prominent physical features. Henry Taylor is reputed to have said: 'It is to my mind one of the greatest triumphs of photography . . . that Sir John Herschel's face has been perpetuated, so that future generations, as well as the present, may see it in all its grandeur and dignity.' Herschel himself preferred the photograph on page 23: '. . . the one of the old Paterfamilias with his black cap on is, I think, the climax of Photographic Art and beats everything I have ever liked in photography before'. This message is inscribed on the mount of the print in the Royal Photographic Society's Collection. The photograph on page 24 is the least well known but is a brilliant representation nonetheless, with emphasis on the upturned eyes, with their steadfast gaze, as though concentrating on some distant star.

Thomas Carlyle was photographed by Julia Cameron at Little Holland House at the time Watts began his painting of the historian. The painter completed his portrait of Carlyle in the succeeding year in which the great Victorian was photographed by Mrs Cameron. The comparison between painting (page 20) and photographs (pages 20 and 21) is an interesting one. Watts was more inspired by allegorical and narrative subjects than by formal portraiture. In this instance the painting is probably a good likeness but lacks interpretation of qualities of mind and spirit, the hands being the dominant feature. The photographs, however, express the inner conflicts which assailed Thomas Carlyle, especially the full face portrait (page 21). The head was lit with ruthless intensity, revealing certain aspects of character but concealing others. This portrait has been likened to 'a rough block of Michael Angelo's sculpture'. There is a tenderness and yet an infinite sadness manifest in the profile (page 20) to which Roger Fry referred in his Introduction to *Victorian Pictures of Famous Men and Fair Women*: 'Neither Whistler nor Watts . . . approach the poignancy of this revelation of character.' Carlyle's comment on the full face study was blunt: 'It is as if suddenly the picture began to speak, terrifically ugly and woe-begone, but it has something of a likeness —my candid opinion.' In some of the prints made of the full face portrait the modelling light comes from the left whilst in others it comes from the right. Both prints are from the same negative image. It is most likely that one or other are single transfer carbon prints in which the image has been laterally reversed.

Julia Cameron took more photographs of Sir Henry Taylor than of any other male sitter. She called him 'Philip' after *Philip van Artevelde,* the hero of his poetic drama, often to the embarrassment of his family and her friends. He was a highly placed government official at the Colonial Office where he was offered the Under-Secretaryship. As he considered his poetry to be of greater importance than his

continued on page 56

THE
PHOTOGRAPHS

Top Ellen Terry, 1864

Below Profile of a Lady, 1861. A pencil drawing by Dante Gabriel Rossetti (The Victoria and Albert Museum)

'The Dirty Monk' (Alfred, Lord Tennyson), 1865

Top 'Red and White Roses' (Kate and Elizabeth 'Topsy' Keown), 1865
Below 'Lilies' (a Renaissance theme with Mary Hillier and Elizabeth 'Topsy' Keown), 1865

Top 'Sisters', 1865

Below 'My Grandchild' sometimes captioned 'Devotion' (Mary Hillier with Archie Cameron), 1865

Top 'Blackberry Gathering' (Mary Ryan, Kate Keown and unidentified boy in sailor suit), c.1865
Below 'Paul and Virginia' (Freddy Gould and Elizabeth 'Topsy' Keown), 1865

Left 'April Love', 1856. Painting by Arthur Hughes (Tate Gallery)
Right 'Daisies Pied' (possibly Kate Keown), 1865–6

The poet Robert Browning, 1866

The poet Henry Wadsworth Longfellow, 1868

Julia Jackson, wife of Herbert Duckworth, niece of Julia Cameron, 1867

'The Mountain Nymph, Sweet Liberty' (Cyllene Wilson), 1866

Left Thomas Carlyle, 1868. A painting by George Frederick Watts (The Victoria and Albert Museum)

Right Thomas Carlyle, Scottish essayist, historian and philosopher, 1867

Thomas Carlyle, 1867

Charles Hay Cameron, Julia Cameron's husband, 1869

Sir John Herschel, with beret, 1867

'The Astronomer' (Sir John Herschel), 1867

Sir John Herschel, 1867

Philosopher and poet Sir Henry Taylor. Study in the manner of Rembrandt, c.1867

Sir Henry Taylor, 1867

Alfred, Lord Tennyson, Poet Laureate, 1869

'The Dream', known as 'The Daydream' (Mary Hillier), 1869

Mrs Ewen Cameron (formerly Miss Annie Chinery): 'Our Beautiful Birdie, my Ewen's Bride of 18th November, 1869'

Mrs Ewen Cameron, sometimes captioned 'Balaustrion', c.1869

'The Letter Writer' (May Prinsep), 1870

Andrew L. Hitchins, husband of May Prinsep, 1874

Top Mrs Duckworth (Julia Jackson) with Florence Fisher (niece of Julia Cameron) and two boys (possibly Gerald and George, the sons of Mrs Duckworth)

Below 'In the Garden', 1867

34

'The Whisper of the Muse' (G.F. Watts, Freddie Gould and Elizabeth 'Topsy' Keown), c.1867

Top 'Too late! Too late!', 1868
Below 'Rosa Triplex', 1867. Red chalk drawing by Dante Gabriel Rossetti (Tate Gallery)

'Peace, Love and Faith', sometimes captioned 'The Three Sisters', 1868

Left 'Paolo and Francesca da Rimini', (left side of triptych). Drawing by Dante Gabriel Rossetti (Tate Gallery)
Right The Kiss of Peace (reproduced from badly faded print)

'The Kiss of Peace' (Florence Anson on left and Cyllene Wilson on right), 1869

'The Angel at the Sepulchre' (Cyllene Wilson), c.1869

May Prinsep (niece of Thoby Prinsep, Julia Cameron's brother-in-law), 1870

'Choosing' (Ellen Terry), c.1864. Painting by George Frederick Watts (National Portrait Gallery)

'Alethia' (Alice Liddell), 1872

'Pomona' (Alice Liddell), 1872

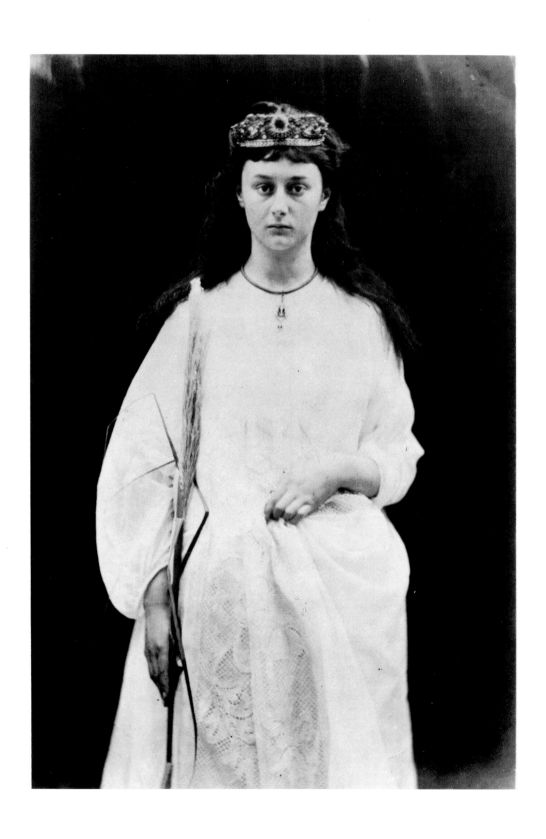

'St. Agnes' (Alice Liddell), 1872

'Prayer' (Florence Anson), c.1872

'Rachel and Laura' (Rachel and Laura Gurney), 1872

Left 'Death Crowning Innocence', 1886–7. Painting by George Frederick Watts (Tate Gallery)

Right 'Venus Chiding Cupid and Removing His Wings', 1873

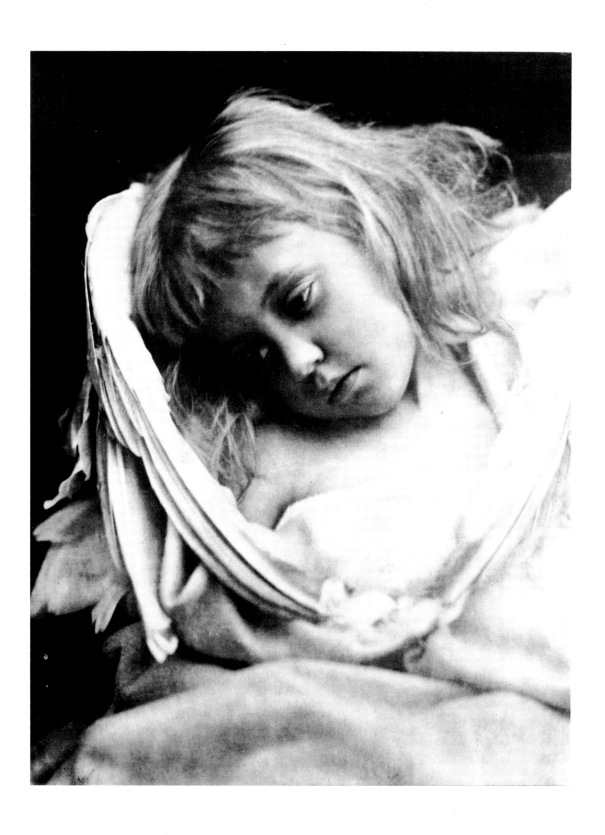

'The Nestling Angel', 1870

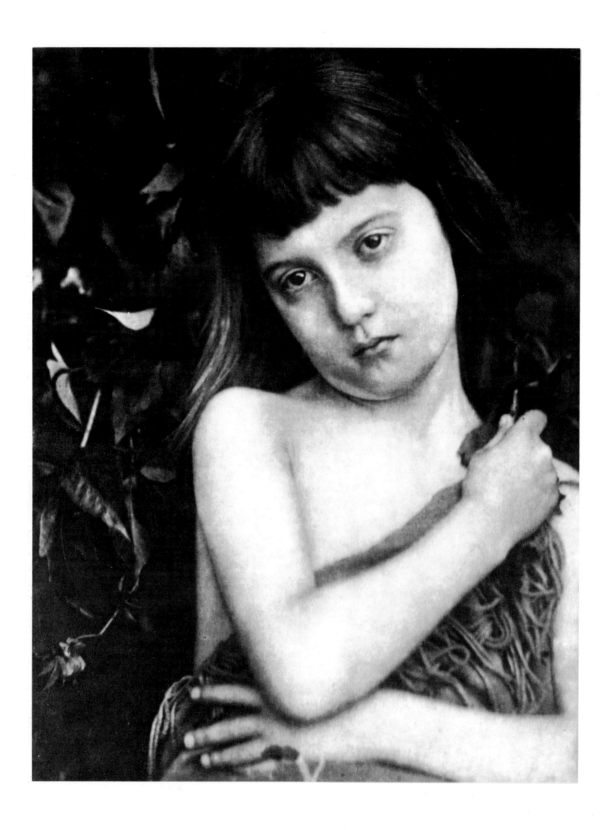

'St. John the Baptist' (Florence Fisher), 1872

Idylls of the King, volume 1, plate 5, 'Vivien and Merlin' (Charles Hay Cameron and a lady visitor to Freshwater), 1874

Idylls of the King, volume 1, plate 8, `Elaine' (May Prinsep) watching the shield of Lancelot, 1874

Idylls of the King, volume 1, plate 4, 'And Enid Sang' (Emily Peacock), 1874

Top: Idylls of the King, volume 1, plate 13, 'The Passing of Arthur' (William Warder), 1874

Below: Idylls of the King, volume 1, plate 10, 'The Parting of Lancelot and Guinevere' (William Warder and May Prinsep), 1874

Group of Kalutara Peasants, Ceylon, 1878

continued from page 8

Civil Service career he refused the post. He stayed at Dimbola each year for two weeks at a time in both spring and autumn. *Sir Henry Taylor* (page 26) is an example of her use of lighting to reveal certain facial features, conceal others, and to create dramatic intensity. She was unafraid of causing impenetrable shadows where she wished to obscure detail. Her contemporaries would not have dared to produce such a photograph, let alone exhibit it. *Sir Henry Taylor* (page 27) is one of her finest portraits with emphasis on the character as well as the features. It is aesthetically impressive and technically good. The plastic qualities are really remarkable, achieved by the subtle relationship between the sharp and diffused parts of the image. It could be said to be a 'speaking likeness' of the poet, who gazed resolutely into the camera lens.

Other of Julia Cameron's characteristics were her magnanimity and great generosity in her dealings with people. Her first reaction on achieving her 'first success' in photography was to search her house to find suitable small gifts for the little Freshwater girl, Annie Philpot, who she believed was responsible for her first successful portrait study after many trials and disappointments with less disciplined and responsive sitters. This spirit of generosity is reflected in particular in her imagery of women. Julia Margaret was the only plain one of the Pattle sisters and three of them were very beautiful. All the sisters were blessed with intelligence and wit. Julia made up for her physical short-comings with her strength of personality, conversational ability and charm. Many women of similar countenance would have been resentful of the beauty of others but Julia was passionately in love with beauty, an emotion which drove her inexorably to an admiration for the Pre-Raphaelite painters and an understanding of the motivation which led to their particular interpretation of the Ideal in womanly form. She strove to idealize feminine beauty through the realistic medium of photography. For this purpose she selected models who combined delicate and clear-cut features in an oval face with wavy abundant long hair and graceful slim figure. Her models bore striking resemblances to those used by the Pre-Raphaelite painters—Dante Gabriel Rossetti in particular—and to her close friend G.F. Watts, the early Symbolist painter.

In this context her early photograph of *Ellen Terry, 1864* (page 10) is of interest. Ellen was photographed by Julia at Sarah Prinsep's home, Little Holland House, and by all accounts was a lively spirited girl who married Watts, many years her senior, at the age of 16. (They were separated after sixteen months of marriage, against her will.) Her portrayal by Mrs Cameron as a demure and modest young woman, with downcast eyes, is out of character. It has been said that this attitude was wishful thinking based on the 'ideal' wife desired by Watts, who treated her like a child. Alternatively it could have been a contemplative pose based on portrait drawings by Dante Gabriel Rossetti, such as *The Profile* (page 10). The downcast head, the delineation of the profile, the rendition of the hair and the pensive thoughtful expression can be seen in Mrs Cameron's photographs time and again, all of which are typical of Rossetti's portrayal of women.

There were many beautiful young women within Julia's circle of relatives, friends and neighbours. Julia Duckworth (neé Jackson), her niece, daughter of her sister Maria, was a great beauty with swan-like neck, oval face and delicate features. She was photographed many times, with mixed success and failure. The profile study

Her contemporaries would not have dared to produce such a photograph, let alone exhibit it.

(page 18) is one of the best. The model Julia Cameron preferred to all others for the portrayal of 'ideal' mothers in Renaissance type themes and illustrations of religious subjects was one of her parlourmaids, Mary Hillier, who also acted as one of her photographic assistants. She was the principal figure in *Lilies* (page 12). There are several variants on this theme which include a Madonna and child, one of which is titled *The Annunciation*. Mary Hillier was also the earthly 'mother' in *My Grandchild (Devotion)* (page 13), and the symbolic figure in the photograph captioned *The Dream* (page 29). Known as *The Daydream* this photograph was thought to be 'quite divine!' by G.F. Watts, who made this statement on the mount of the photograph and added his signature. An interesting aesthetic effect was produced by the rendition of the hair. Julia Cameron focused the 760 mm (30-inch) lens on the profile which is tolerably sharp whilst other features are diffused, most noticeably the beautiful hair which softly ripples over Mary's shoulders. Mary was known on the Isle of Wight as 'Mary Madonna' and 'Island Mary' because of her roles in front of the camera.

Another favourite model within the Cameron household was Mary Ryan, the daughter of a beggar woman whom Mrs Cameron met by chance on Putney Heath and adopted, educating Mary with her two youngest sons, and employing her as a parlourmaid when she grew up. Mary Ryan had a rare beauty and a sweet nature and married a high ranking member of the Indian Civil Service becoming Lady Cotton. She first met her future husband when she was selling prints of Mrs Cameron's photographs at an exhibition displayed at Colnaghi's. She was an inspiration to the photographer and was featured in several of her illustrative photographs such as *Blackberry Gathering* (page 14), and *The Gardener's Daughter*. Although the former photograph is based on a very carefully planned composition within the traditions of painting it is freer and more spontaneous in effect than the work of most photographers of the period.

Julia Margaret Cameron was essentially an illustrator, her ambition being to pictorially represent the beautiful, romantic and tragic figures of legend, Bible story and contemporaneous poetry. Her imagination was aroused by the Knights of the Round Table and other noble themes. She found inspiration through her friendships with poets and painters. She encouraged amateur dramatics in her own house and doubtless some ideas for her illustrative photographs stemmed from these performances. She said that G.F. Watts 'gave me wings to fly with' and he certainly took every opportunity to encourage and praise her endeavours. In a moment of enthusiasm she threw a cloak round his shoulders and photographed him with Freddie Gould as the little 'Muse' and Elizabeth Keown as the 'cherub' in her charming study, *The Whisper of the Muse* (page 35).

We must compare her imagery with that of certain painters . . . Rossetti, Watts.

To understand Mrs Cameron's illustrative photography it is necessary to compare her imagery with that of certain painters, especially D.G. Rossetti and G.F. Watts, and to read the relevant passages from the poems of Tennyson. She was particularly fond of *April Love* by Arthur Hughes (page 15) and this may have led to her use of the creeper covered walls of Dimbola and the garden shrubbery as backgrounds for many of her photographs (pages 14, 15, 34, 35, 36, 37, 43, 44, 50). Most are interesting and a few are superb. *In the Garden* (page 34) was probably taken to illustrate Tennyson's poem, *Maud* (Part 1: XIV):

> Maud has a garden of roses
> And lilies fair on a lawn;

There she walks in her state

And tends upon bed and bower . . .

The association of a typical 'English rose', as Mrs Cameron would have regarded the lovely girl she photographed, with the real climbing roses in the garden of Dimbola puts this picture into the context of Tennyson's poem. *Too late! Too late!* (page 36) was also taken to illustrate *Maud* (Part 1: XXII):

She is coming, my dove, my dear;

She is coming my life, my fate;

The red rose cries, 'She is near, she is near:'

And the white rose weeps, 'She is late:'

The larkspur listens, 'I hear, I hear:'

And the lily whispers, 'I wait.'

'The Red Rose' kneels, looking expectant, in the forefront; 'The White Rose' on the right facing inwards, leans on her companion's shoulder; 'The Larkspur' with arms upraised is alert and listening; and 'The Lily' with head bowed in reverence, awaits the coming of Maud, but as the narrative proceeds it becomes evident that it is too late! This photograph is sometimes mistaken for another titled *The Rosebud Garden of Girls* which illustrates the previous verse of *Maud,* Part 1: XXII and in which 'the flowers' of the poem are girls clad in shimmering garments, grouped against a background of climbing roses. That picture was constructed to give a greater feeling of rhythmic activity than the very rigid arrangement of the girls in *Too late! Too late!* although the latter is the better composition of the two.

Peace, Love and Faith (page 37) is an interesting composition, taken as part of a larger group. It has certain correspondences with Rossetti's drawing, *Rosa Triplex* (page 36), both in arrangement and in underlying theme. In the photograph the central girl with her eyes turned towards heaven and the one on the left with lowered head and meek expression are particularly reminiscent of Mrs Cameron's instructions to her various nieces to read the Bible before they went to parties, so that they would be filled with pure thoughts and in the 'right' frame of mind! She doubtless insisted that her models for this photograph followed the same procedure before posing!

The Pre-Raphaelite influence is clearly visible in *The Kiss of Peace* (page 39) which was well conceived and beautifully executed. The two heads were lit to perfection so that the tonalities in the prime print provide a range of 'in-depth' qualities unsurpassed in any of her other photographs. The idea could have been taken from the detail of *Paolo and Francesca da Rimini* by D.G. Rossetti (page 38) but it possesses innocent and demure qualities which the sensuous rhythmic drawing lacks. The melancholy expressions in this and many other Cameron photographs are not due to lengthy exposure times but based on the Pre-Raphaelite notion of ethereal beauty.

Alice Liddell as Alethia . . . *one of the finest of Cameron portraits.*

The splendid portrayal of Alice Liddell as *Alethia* (page 43) is one of the finest of Cameron portraits. (Alice was the subject of Lewis Carroll's famous children's story, *Alice in Wonderland,* and posed before his camera when she was a child.) The association between her head and shoulders and the lace cap hydrangeas and camellia foliage against which she is standing is fascinating. The interplay between sharpness and diffusion of definition in the image is most effective with a finely delineated profile, hair flowing like softly running water and flowers revealed in detail without being obtrusive. It closely resembles *Choosing* by G.F. Watts (page

58

42) in which the decorative values are enhanced by the association of face and hands with camellias and their foliage. The two media have been used to produce nearly identical images in aesthetic terms, although the painting is in colour and the photograph is monochromatic. It is also worth comparing *Choosing,* which is a portrait of Ellen Terry featuring the precocious liveliness of Watts's young wife mirrored in her upturned face, with the sedate portrait of her by Julia Cameron (page 10). Another photograph of Alice Liddell—*St. Agnes* (page 45)—should be studied in conjunction with Tennyson's poem, *St. Agnes' Eve.* The strong frontal pose against a plain black background suggests 'Light' versus 'Darkness', symbolic of the religious theme portrayed:

> Deep on the convent-roof the snows
> Are sparkling to the moon:
> My breath to Heaven like vapour goes:
> May my soul follow soon!
>
> . . .
>
> Draw me, thy bride, a glittering star,
> In raiment white and clean,
>
> . . .

The illustration of Tennyson's *Idylls of the King* was Mrs Cameron's major project. The poet himself suggested that she might consider illustrating the poems he had composed under this title. She embarked upon this formidable task with all her usual energetic determination in 1874 and spent three months on production. She took 200 photographs to obtain the 12 illustrations required, and the hiring of models and armour cost her 'a great deal' of money which she could ill afford. What should have been the peak of her achievement was, in fact, amongst the least rewarding of her efforts. She attempted an interpretation which was too literal and the exercise became an extension of the charades which were such a popular form of amusement in the evenings at Dimbola. Although one or two of the illustrations have charm, others are banal and none are convincing. One of the more pleasing, because it is unpretentious, is *The Parting of Lancelot and Guinevere* (page 54). *And Enid Sang* (page 53) also has its charm, but *The Passing of Arthur* (page 54) is clumsy and comic rather than solemn.

Mrs Cameron took few photographs in Ceylon between 1875 and her death in 1879 and those she did take were more in the nature of documentary portraiture than her former style. She wrote on the mount of *Group of Kalutara Peasants* (page 55), 'The girl is twelve, the old man says he is her father and is one hundred years old!'.

Her photographs, as photographic images, are unique. No-one before or since has produced a range of portraits which bear any resemblance to hers, and although many other photographers practised illustrative photography in the Victorian era her work is outstandingly different from that of others. Her aims in photography were very clear, as stated in *Annals of My Glass House*: 'I longed to arrest all beauty that came before me, and at length the longing has been satisfied . . .', and in reference to Carlyle, 'When I have had such great men before my camera my whole soul has endeavoured to do its duty towards them in recording faithfully the greatness of the inner as well as the features of the outer man. The photograph thus taken has been almost the embodiment of a prayer.'

'I longed to arrest all beauty that came before me,' she wrote.

Technical note

Studio: Mrs Cameron converted a glazed hen-house into a glass house (daylight) studio for portraiture and illustrative photography. It was described by a sitter as 'very untidy and very uncomfortable'. In the summer months she took many of her illustrative photographs and some portraits out of doors in the garden of Dimbola (her house), against walls covered with climbing plants or with shrubs as background. When she held a portrait session at her sister Sarah's home, Little Holland House in London, she used the studio of the painter, G.F. Watts, for the purpose.

Props: Apart from a simple chair no supports for the body or limbs were used although professional photographers of the time used posing stools, head clamps, and arm rests. Neither did 'background props' play any role in Mrs Cameron's photographs. She occasionally included domestic articles such as a poker, and amateur theatrical accessories such as a black cloak or cloth, shawls and head coverings.

Lighting: The majority of photographers used daylight for portraiture during this period and Mrs Cameron was no exception. She controlled the light in her studio with roller-blinds which admitted shafts of light rather than a large expanse of flat lighting. This control enabled her to obtain chiaroscuro effects or top and side lighting instead of a uniform flood of light. All sitters were treated individually and she made no attempt to develop a standardized lighting technique.

Cameras and lenses: Her first camera consisted of two wooden boxes, one sliding within the other by a rack and pinion movement. It was made to take plates of size 23 × 28 cm (9 × 11 inches). On two separate occasions in 1980–1 a box designed to hold glass negatives of this size, said to have belonged to Mrs Cameron, has been sold at auction in London.

She received a lens for this camera as a present from her daughter, Julia, as stated in her *Annals*. It was a *Jamin* lens of French manufacture which was reported by Thomas Ross Dallmeyer (who was requested to examine it by Dr P.H. Emerson in 1890) as having a focal length of 305 mm (12 inches) and a diameter of 76 mm (3 inches). It had a fixed aperture of f/6–7. It suffered from chromatic aberration. Mrs Cameron used the *Jamin* lens and the camera for her photographs between 1864 and some date in 1866 and occasionally thereafter. The focal length of the lens was too short for the plate size for 'head and shoulders' portraiture but as all her early photographs are half-, three-quarters- or full-length studies, distortion is not unduly noticeable, with the exception of hands if placed in front of the body line (as with *The Dirty Monk* portrait of Tennyson, page 11). She was probably unaware of the defects of this lens and stated her preference for focusing visually: 'When focusing and coming to something which to my eye was very beautiful, I stopped there instead of screwing on the lens to the more definite focus which all other photographers insist on.' However the lens aberration made it virtually impossible for her to obtain the sharp image quality of the professional photographers by studying the visual appearance of the image on the ground glass screen. This factor accounts for the variations in sharpness of definition (from moderately sharp to out of focus) in her early photographs, in addition to the 'blur' caused by movement by the sitter during the long exposures needed.

In the spring of 1866 Mrs Cameron bought a larger camera which took 30 × 38 cm (12 × 15 inch) plates. It was fitted with a Rapid Rectilinear lens of 760 mm (30 inch) focal length and aperture of f/8. (The lens was recommended by Dallmeyer, the designer, for use with 40 × 50 cm (16 × 20 inch) plates.) By using this combination Mrs Cameron guarded against distortion in her 'close-up' studies, but the depth of field—the range of sharp focus—was greatly reduced. The long focal length and 'controlled' light in her studio made very lengthy exposures (two to six minutes in her studio) at full aperture inevitable. This technique resulted in a sharp focus over a limited part of the subject only, which was usually the eyes and mouth, or the edge of the face in profile studies, the rest of the features being unsharp to a greater or lesser extent. The lengthy exposures also resulted in some 'blurring' from slight to very noticeable according to the ability or otherwise of the sitter to keep absolutely still.

In spite of the disadvantages the merit of this 'lens-plate' size combination was that her imagery assumed plastic, rounded qualities not to be found in the work of other photographers who used less formidable equipment. This technical factor made an important contribution to the aesthetic appeal of her photographs.

Darkroom: She converted a coal-house, which was a 'lean-to' extension in an angle between two main walls of the house, into a darkroom but the water had to be drawn from the well nearby. This little room was adjacent to the glass house studio.

Negative making: Mrs Cameron lacked technical training and, moreover, had a cavalier disregard for the accepted standards of photographic technique. For example she received a distressed warning from her friend, Sir John Herschel: '. . . that dreadful poison the cyanide of potassium—letting it run over your hands so profusely—Pray! Pray! be more cautious.'

Mrs Cameron with her three darkroom assistants—her maids Ellen Ottington, Mary Hillier and Kate Shepherd—used the wet collodion process for making negatives. The size and weight of the glass plates must have posed some problems in the tasks of coating, sensitizing, developing and fixing. Being impatient of technicalities she ignored unevenness of coating, spots caused by airbells, dust speck marks and even gashes in the collodion film, provided the image was as she wished it to be. Varnishing, an essential last step in the process, was a tricky business and it is said that she lost 45 good negatives due to the cracking of the collodion after its subjection to varnish.

Print making: She made 'print out' silver prints by contact from her negatives, using commercially prepared albumenized paper which she had to sensitize with silver chloride before printing. In her correspondence there are no more than two or three passing references to her printing technique. In *Annals of my Glass House* she describes her excitement on achieving her 'first success' and adds, 'I printed, toned, fixed and framed it and presented it to her father that same day'. In a letter to Sir Edward Ryan in 1874 she described how each print made for the *Idylls* publication was subjected to nine cans of water from the well 'in freezing weather' (December) in order to wash it properly. Although both these brief sentences imply a careful regard for printing procedures the evidence does not support the inference.

It is reasonable to assume that she, herself, made the prints for the albums which she presented to relatives and friends (such as *The Herschel Album* acquired by the National Portrait Gallery of London and the album presented to her sister 'Mia' which was acquired by a private collector—both

within the last decade). It is certain that she produced the prints for the advance copies, at least, of *The Idylls of the King,* published by Henry S. King and Company—the edition which contained photographic prints, full size, of her photographs. Prints in all these albums show considerable deterioration, some having faded very badly indeed. The variation in print size, which could cause misunderstanding, is due to the variation in margin which she allowed at the edges of plates for handling during coating and processing.

There is considerable variation in print quality in Julia Margaret Cameron's photographs, now that they have been subjected to the test of time. The best are few in number and can be considered as 'prime' prints. The richness and beauty of these prints has to be seen to be believed. They are toned albumen prints, the mount bearing her usual signature and statement. (Her 'signature' is not positive proof that she made the print herself as at times pressure of work required her assistants to sign photographs on her behalf, which accounts for variations in the writing). It is by no means certain that she made all or any of the 'prime' prints. It is known that many prints were made for her by P. & D. Colnaghi's, the print sellers, who set up a photographic printing department in 1857. The majority of the albumen prints made from her negatives range from acceptable quality with minimum fading round the edges to very badly faded to a light sulphur yellow or with blotches of different colours and densities throughout the print. All the photographs sold by Colnaghi's on her behalf bear their blind-stamp on the mounts. They are inscribed by Mrs Cameron: 'From life. Copyright Registered Photograph. Julia Margaret Cameron.' In some instances there is a date and additional remarks and well known sitters sometimes added their autograph. It is

also possible that Colnaghi's made prints for her to present to friends and sitters which do not bear their blind-stamp.

Before leaving England for Ceylon in 1875 Mrs Cameron entered into an arrangement with the Autotype Company, who specialized in carbon printing, whereby she deposited her negatives with them so that permanent (carbon) prints could be made from them for sale to the public. It was also agreed that the Company could make copy negatives from the originals. This accounts for size variations in some of the photographs as the copy negatives could be larger or smaller than the originals. None of the prints made by the Autotype Company after the Camerons' departure for Ceylon are signed. Some of the carbon prints give a better impression of what the original silver prints must have looked like than many of the remaining silver prints which are so badly faded.

In addition to using her own facilities for print making Mrs Cameron occasionally made prints in the photographic department of the South Kensington Museum (now the Victoria and Albert Museum). As the facilities would have been better than her own with the big advantage of running water available she could have made her prime prints there.

Retouching: Mrs Cameron proudly wrote 'untouched' beneath some of her photographs. She did not acknowledge the difference between so-called 'improvement' retouching of the image, by which it was possible to remove unsightly facial characteristics such as 'moles', and the removal of spots and blemishes caused by inadequate photographic technique. Some concession to the latter would have added to the undoubted aesthetic of many of her finest photographs. The worst blemishes were removed by the Autotype Company from the carbon prints which they made.

Chronology

1815
Born at Garden Reach, Calcutta, on 11 June, to James and Adeline Pattle.

1818
Educated in Paris and England between 1818 and 1834.

1838
Married Charles Hay Cameron in Calcutta, India.

1839
Birth of eldest child, named Julia.

1840
Birth of eldest son, second child, named Eugene Hay.
In succeeding years four sons were born: Hardinge Hay, Ewen Hay, Charles Hay, and Henry Herschel Hay. The last named, the youngest, was the only child to follow in his mother's footsteps. He practised as a professional photographer between c.1885 and c.1905.

1848
Returned to England from India on the retirement of husband and took up residence at Ephraim Court, Tunbridge Wells, Kent.

1850
Moved home to Sheen Lodge, East Sheen, London.

1854
Moved home to Ashburton Cottage, Putney Heath, London.

1860
Shortly after Charles Cameron's return from visit to Ceylon the Cameron household moved to 'Dimbola' on the Isle of Wight.

1863
Charles Cameron in the Indian sub-continent once again.
Julia Cameron took up photography in December, after daughter and son-in-law gave her a camera and a Jamin lens.

1864
Took her first successful photograph in January. Presented photograph album to G.F. Watts in February, containing her earliest 'successes'.
Became a member of the Photographic Society of Great Britain (RPS) in June.

1865
One-woman show of photographs at Colnaghi's, print sellers, London, from November 1865 to January 1866.

1866
One-woman show at the French Gallery, London, from December 1866 to January 1867.

1867
Took many of her finest portraits in this year—Herschel, Taylor, Carlyle.

1868
Charles Darwin photographed at Dimbola. One-woman show at the German Gallery, London, in January and February. In summer took photographs to illustrate Tennyson's *Maud* and other poems.

1874
Started writing *Annals of My Glass House* which was first published in 1889, unfinished.
Embarked on the illustrations for Tennyson's *Idylls of the King*.
29 November: first of the twelve volumes of the Cabinet edition of *The Idylls of the King* published, illustrated with woodcuts made from Mrs Cameron's photographs.
c. 20 December: copies of Alfred Tennyson's *The Idylls of the King and Other Poems, Illustrated by Julia Margaret Cameron, volume 1* first published under imprint of Henry S. King and Company of 65 Cornhill, London. The folio volume was bound in red half-morocco and contained twelve signed and titled illustrations to the poems, mounted on blue-grey card, with *The Dirty Monk* (Alfred, Lord Tennyson) as a frontispiece. The photographs were inter-leaved with excerpts from the poems, lithographed from Mrs Cameron's handwriting.

1875
May: second similar but rarer volume illustrating twelve different scenes from *The Idylls of the King and Other Poems*, with the same photograph of Tennyson as a frontispiece, was published.
October: Mr and Mrs Cameron moved to Ceylon.

1878
May: a month's visit to England.

1879
26 January: Julia Margaret Cameron died at the age of sixty three and was buried in Ceylon. Her huIband survived her by sixteen months and died at the age of eighty five.

References and Bibliography

Cameron, Julia Margaret. *Annals of My Glass House.* The Royal Photographic Society's *Journal*, July, 1927.
Cameron, Julia Margaret. *Illustrations to Idylls of the King and Other Poems*, volume 1, 1874 and volume 2, 1875.
Emerson, Peter Henry. Essay accompanied by four of her photographs printed in photogravure in *Sun Artists,* Kegal, Paul and Trench, 1891.
Ford, Colin. *The Herschel Album,* 1975, National Portrait Gallery, London.
Ford, Colin. *The Cameron Collection,* 1981, National Portrait Gallery, London.
Gernsheim, Helmut. *Julia Margaret Cameron, Her Life and Photographic Work,* 1975, Aperture, Millerton, New York.
Hunt, William Holman. *Pre-Raphaelitism and the Pre-Raphaelite Brotherhood,* 1905.
Ovenden, Graham. *A Victorian Album, Julia Margaret Cameron and Her Circle.* Introductory Essay by Lord David Cecil, 1975, Secker and Warburg.
The Oxford Book of English Mystical Verse
Tennyson, Alfred. *In Memoriam, Maud and Other Poems,* 1974, J.M. Dent & Sons.
Tennyson's Verse, selected with an introduction by Lord David Cecil, 1971, Faber and Faber.
Watts, Mary Seton. *George Frederick Watts,* London, 1912.
Woolf, Virginia, and Fry, Roger. *Victorian Photographs of Famous Men and Fair Women,* London, 1926.

All the illustrations of Cameron photographs in this volume have been reproduced from original photographs in the Collection of The Royal Photographic Society.
The reproductions of paintings and drawings in this volume are by kind permission of the following: The Tate Gallery, London: pages 15, 36, 38 and 48; The National Portrait Gallery, London: page 42; The Victoria and Albert Museum: pages 10 and 20.

Index of
photographs

Author

Margaret Harker was Head of the School of Photography in the Polytechnic of Central London between 1959 and 1975, when she became a Pro Rector of the Polytechnic until her retirement in 1980. She has been a practising professional photographer as well as a teacher of photography, and is a photographic historian. She is internationally known for her lectures and writings on the art of photography, photographic history, and education.

Presently the Chairman of the Photography Board of the Council for National Academic Awards, Professor Harker is also an Honorary Fellow of the Royal Photographic Society and the Institute of Incorporated Photographers, and has been President of both organizations. She is an Honorary Fellow of the British Kinematograph, Sound and Television Society, a Corresponding Member of the Deutsche Gesellschaft für Photographie, and Vice President of the European Society for the History of Photography.

Professor Harker's previous publications include *Victorian and Edwardian Photographs*; *The Linked Ring, the Secession in Photography 1892–1910*; and *Photographing Architecture*.

Series Consultant Editors

Romeo Martinez has worked in photographic journalism for over 50 years. Resident in Paris, he is the author of several books on the history of photography and is the editor of the *Bibliothek der Photographie* series. He was responsible for the relaunch on the international market of the magazine *Camera*. From 1957 to 1965, he organized the biennial photographic exhibitions in Venice. Romeo Martinez organized the iconographic department at the Pompidou Centre in Paris. He is a member of the Administration Council and of the Art Commission of the Societé Français de Photographie and a member of the Deutsche Gesellschaft für Photographie.

Bryn Campbell has been active both as a professional photographer and as an editor and writer on photography. He is known to many as the presenter of the BBC TV series *Exploring Photography*. As a photographer, he has worked for a Fleet Street agency, with *The Observer,* and on assignments for *Geo* and *The Observer Magazine*. He has been Assistant Editor of *Practical Photography* and of *Photo News Weekly,* Editor of *Cameras & Equipment,* Deputy Editor of *The British Journal of Photography* and, from 1964 to 1966, Picture Editor of *The Observer*.

In 1974 he was made an Honorary Associate Lecturer in Photographic Arts at the Polytechnic of Central London. The same year he was appointed a Trustee of the Photographers' Gallery, London. He served on the Photography Sub-Committee of the Arts Council and later became a member of the Art Panel. He is a Fellow of the Institute of Incorporated Photographers and a Fellow of the Royal Photographic Society. His book *World Photography* was published in 1981.

First published in 1983 by
William Collins Sons & Co Ltd

London · Glasgow · Sydney
Auckland · Johannesburg

© 1982 Gruppo Editoriale Fabbri S.p.A.,
Milan

ISBN 0 00 411937 1

Typesetting by Chambers Wallace, London
Printed in Italy